SIR GAWAIN AND THE GREEN KNIGHT

TECHNICAL DIRECTOR Maxwell Krohn
EDITORIAL DIRECTOR Justin Kestler
MANAGING EDITOR Ben Florman

SERIES EDITORS Boomie Aglietti, Justin Kestler
PRODUCTION Christian Lorentzen, Camille Murphy

WRITERS Rebecca Gaines, Holly Barbaccia
EDITORS Benjamin Morgan, Sarah Friedberg

This edition published by Spark Publishing

Spark Publishing
A Division of SparkNotes LLC
120 Fifth Avenue, 8th Floor
New York, NY 10011

02 03 04 05 SN 9 8 7 6 5 4 3 2 1

Please send all comments and questions or report errors to
feedback@sparknotes.com.

Library of Congress information available upon request

Printed and bound in the United States

RRD-C

ISBN 1-58663-489-5

INTRODUCTION: STOPPING TO BUY SPARKNOTES ON A SNOWY EVENING

Whose words these are you *think* you know.
Your paper's due tomorrow, though;
We're glad to see you stopping here
To get some help before you go.

Lost your course? You'll find it here.
Face tests and essays without fear.
Between the words, good grades at stake:
Get great results throughout the year.

Once school bells caused your heart to quake
As teachers circled each mistake.
Use SparkNotes and no longer weep,
Ace every single test you take.

Yes, books are lovely, dark, and deep,
But only what you grasp you keep,
With hours to go before you sleep,
With hours to go before you sleep.

CONTENTS

NOTE: This SparkNote refers to Marie Boroff's translation of *Sir Gawain and the Green Knight*, published in the Norton Anthology of English Literature, Volume 1, edited by M. H. Abrams.

CONTEXT

T HE ALLITERATIVE POEM *Sir Gawain and the Green Knight,* likely written in the mid to late fourteenth century, survives in a late-fourteenth-century manuscript with three other poems—Pearl, Purity, and Patience— by the same author. Very little is known about the author of these poems, but most scholars believe him to have been a university-trained clerk or the official of a provincial estate (this SparkNote refers to him as the "Pearl-poet" or the "Gawain-poet"). Though it cannot be said with certainty that one person wrote all four poems, some shared characteristics point toward common authorship and also suggest that the Gawain-poet may have written another poem, called St. Erkenwald, that exists in a separate manuscript. All the poems except *Sir Gawain and the Green Knight* deal with overtly Christian subject matter, and it remains unclear why Sir Gawain, an Arthurian romance, was included in an otherwise religious manuscript.

Sir Gawain and the Green Knight was written in a dialect of Middle English that links it with Britain's Northwest Midlands, probably the county of Cheshire or Lancashire. The English provinces of the late fourteenth century, although they did not have London's economic, political, and artistic centrality, were not necessarily less culturally active than London, where Geoffrey Chaucer and William Langland were writing at the time. In fact, the works of the Gawain-poet belong to a type of literature traditionally known as the Alliterative Revival, usually associated with northern England. Contrary to what the name of the movement suggests, the alliterative meter of Old English had not actually disappeared and therefore did not need reviving. Nevertheless, *Sir Gawain and the Green Knight* exists as a testament that the style continued well into the fourteenth century, if not in London, then in the provinces.

Sir Gawain and the Green Knight's adapted Old English meter tends to connect the two halves of each poetic line through alliteration, or repetition of consonants. The poem also uses rhyme to structure its stanzas, and each group of long alliterative lines concludes with a word or phrase containing two syllables and a quatrain—known together as the "bob and wheel." The phrase "bob and wheel" derives from a technique used when spinning cloth—the bobs and wheels in *Sir Gawain and the Green Knight* help to spin the plot and narrative together in intricate ways. They provide commentaries on what has just happened, create or fulfill moments of suspense, and serve as transitions to the next scene or idea.

Told in four "fitts," or parts, the poem weaves together at least three separate narrative strings commonly found in medieval folklore and romance. The first plot, the beheading game, appears in ancient folklore and may derive from pagan myths related to the agricultural cycles of planting and harvesting crops. The second and third plots concern the exchange of winnings and the hero's temptation; both of these plots derive from medieval romances and dramatize tests of the hero's honesty, loyalty, and chastity. As the story unfolds, we discover that the three apparently separate plotlines intersect in surprising ways.

A larger story that frames the narrative is that of Morgan le Faye's traditional hatred for Arthur and his court, called Camelot. Morgan, Arthur's half sister and a powerful sorceress, usually appears in legend as an enemy of the Round Table. Indeed, medieval readers knew of Morgan's role in the destined fall of Camelot, the perfect world depicted in *Sir Gawain and the Green Knight*.

The poem's second frame is a historical one. The poem begins and ends with references to the myth of Britain's lineage from the ancient city of Troy, by way of Britain's Trojan founder, Brutus. These references root the Arthurian romance in the tradition of epic literature, older and more elevated than the tradition of courtly literature, and link fourteenth-century England to Rome, which was also founded by a Trojan (Aeneas). Thus, *Sir Gawain and the Green Knight* presents us with a version of translatio imperii—a Latin phrase referring to the transfer of culture from one civilization (classical antiquity, in this case) to another (medieval England). The Gawain-poet at times adopts an ironic tone, but he also displays a deep investment in elevating his country's legends, history, and literary forms—especially Arthurian romance—by relating them directly to classical antiquity.

PLOT OVERVIEW

URING A NEW YEAR'S EVE FEAST at King Arthur's court, a strange figure, referred to only as the Green Knight, pays the court an unexpected visit. He challenges the group's leader or any other brave representative to a game. The Green Knight says that he will allow whomever accepts the challenge to strike him with his own axe, on the condition that the challenger find him in exactly one year to receive a blow in return.

Stunned, Arthur hesitates to respond, but when the Green Knight mocks Arthur's silence, the king steps forward to take the challenge. As soon as Arthur grips the Green Knight's axe, Sir Gawain leaps up and asks to take the challenge himself. He takes hold of the axe and, in one deadly blow, cuts off the knight's head. To the amazement of the court, the now-headless Green Knight picks up his severed head. Before riding away, the head reiterates the terms of the pact, reminding the young Gawain to seek him in a year and a day at the Green Chapel. After the Green Knight leaves, the company goes back to its festival, but Gawain is uneasy.

Time passes, and autumn arrives. On the Day of All Saints, Gawain prepares to leave Camelot and find the Green Knight. He puts on his best armor, mounts his horse, Gringolet, and starts off toward North Wales, traveling through the wilderness of northwest Britain. Gawain encounters all sorts of beasts, suffers from hunger and cold, and grows more desperate as the days pass. On Christmas Day, he prays to find a place to hear Mass, then looks up to see a castle shimmering in the distance. The lord of the castle welcomes Gawain warmly, introducing him to his lady and to the old woman who sits beside her. For sport, the host (whose name is later revealed to be Bertilak) strikes a deal with Gawain: the host will go out hunting with his men every day, and when he returns in the evening, he will exchange his winnings for anything Gawain has managed to acquire by staying behind at the castle. Gawain happily agrees to the pact, and goes to bed.

The first day, the lord hunts a herd of does, while Gawain sleeps late in his bedchambers. On the morning of the first day, the lord's wife sneaks into Gawain's chambers and attempts to seduce him. Gawain puts her off, but before she leaves she steals one kiss from

3

him. That evening, when the host gives Gawain the venison he has captured, Gawain kisses him, since he has won one kiss from the lady. The second day, the lord hunts a wild boar. The lady again enters Gawain's chambers, and this time she kisses Gawain twice. That evening Gawain gives the host the two kisses in exchange for the boar's head.

The third day, the lord hunts a fox, and the lady kisses Gawain three times. She also asks him for a love token, such as a ring or a glove. Gawain refuses to give her anything and refuses to take anything from her, until the lady mentions her girdle. The green silk girdle she wears around her waist is no ordinary piece of cloth, the lady claims, but possesses the magical ability to protect the person who wears it from death. Intrigued, Gawain accepts the cloth, but when it comes time to exchange his winnings with the host, Gawain gives the three kisses but does not mention the lady's green girdle. The host gives Gawain the fox skin he won that day, and they all go to bed happy, but weighed down with the fact that Gawain must leave for the Green Chapel the following morning to find the Green Knight.

New Year's Day arrives, and Gawain dons his armor, including the girdle, then sets off with Gringolet to seek the Green Knight. A guide accompanies him out of the estate grounds. When they reach the border of the forest, the guide promises not to tell anyone if Gawain decides to give up the quest. Gawain refuses, determined to meet his fate head-on. Eventually, he comes to a kind of crevice in a rock, visible through the tall grasses. He hears the whirring of a grindstone, confirming his suspicion that this strange cavern is in fact the Green Chapel. Gawain calls out, and the Green Knight emerges to greet him. Intent on fulfilling the terms of the contract, Gawain presents his neck to the Green Knight, who proceeds to feign two blows. On the third feint, the Green Knight nicks Gawain's neck, barely drawing blood. Angered, Gawain shouts that their contract has been met, but the Green Knight merely laughs.

The Green Knight reveals his name, Bertilak, and explains that he is the lord of the castle where Gawain recently stayed. Because Gawain did not honestly exchange all of his winnings on the third day, Bertilak drew blood on his third blow. Nevertheless, Gawain has proven himself a worthy knight, without equal in all the land. When Gawain questions Bertilak further, Bertilak explains that the old woman at the castle is really Morgan le Faye, Gawain's aunt and King Arthur's half sister. She sent the Green Knight on his original errand and used her magic to change Bertilak's appearance. Relieved to be alive but extremely guilty about his sinful failure to tell the whole truth, Gawain wears the girdle on his arm as a reminder of his own failure. He returns to Arthur's court, where all the knights join Gawain, wearing girdles on their arms to show their support.

CHARACTER LIST

Sir Gawain The story's protagonist, Arthur's nephew and one of his most loyal knights. Although he modestly disclaims it, Gawain has the reputation of being a great knight and courtly lover. He prides himself on his observance of the five points of chivalry in every aspect of his life. Gawain is a pinnacle of humility, piety, integrity, loyalty, and honesty. His only flaw proves to be that he loves his own life so much that he will lie in order to protect himself. Gawain leaves the Green Chapel penitent and changed.

Green Knight A mysterious visitor to Camelot. The Green Knight's huge stature, wild appearance, and green complexion set him apart from the beardless knights and beautiful ladies of Arthur's Camelot. He is an ambiguous figure: he says that he comes in friendship, not wanting to fight, but the friendly game he proposes is quite deadly. He attaches great importance to verbal contracts, expecting Sir Gawain to go to great lengths to hold up his end of their bargain. The Green Knight shows himself to be a supernatural being when he picks up his own severed head and rides out of Arthur's court, still speaking. At the same time, he seems to symbolize the natural world, in that he is killed and reborn as part of a cycle. At the poem's end, we discover that the Green Knight is also Bertilak, Gawain's host, and one of Morgan le Faye's minions.

Bertilak of Hautdesert The sturdy, good-natured lord of the castle where Gawain spends Christmas. We only learn Bertilak's name at the end of *Sir Gawain and the Green Knight*. The poem associates Bertilak with the natural world—his beard resembles a beaver, his face a fire— but also with the courtly behavior of an aristocratic host. Boisterous, powerful, brave, and generous, Lord

7

Bertilak provides an interesting foil to King Arthur. At the end of the poem we learn that Bertilak and the Green Knight are the same person, magically enchanted by Morgan le Faye for her own designs.

Bertilak's wife Bertilak's wife attempts to seduce Gawain on a daily basis during his stay at the castle. Though the poem presents her to the reader as no more than a beautiful young woman, Bertilak's wife is an amazingly clever debater and an astute reader of Gawain's responses as she argues her way through three attempted seductions. Flirtatious and intelligent, Bertilak's wife ultimately turns out to be another pawn in Morgan le Faye's plot.

Morgan le Faye The Arthurian tradition typically portrays Morgan as a powerful sorceress, trained by Merlin, as well as the half sister of King Arthur. Not until the last one hundred lines do we discover that the old woman at the castle is Morgan le Faye and that she has controlled the poem's entire action from beginning to end. As she often does in Arthurian literature, Morgan appears as an enemy of Camelot, one who aims to cause as much trouble for her half brother and his followers as she can.

King Arthur The king of Camelot. In *Sir Gawain and the Green Knight*, Arthur is young and beardless, and his court is in its golden age. Arthur's refusal to eat until he hears a fantastic tale shows the petulance of youth, as does Arthur's initial stunned response to the Green Knight's challenge. However, like a good king, Arthur soon steps forward to take on the challenge. At the story's end, Arthur joins his nephew in wearing a green girdle on his arm, showing that Gawain's trial has taught him about his own fallibility.

Queen Guinevere Arthur's wife. The beautiful young Guinevere of *Sir Gawain and the Green Knight* seems to have little in common with the one of later Arthurian legend. She sits next to Gawain at the New Year's feast and remains a silent, objectified presence in the midst of the knights of the Round Table.

Gringolet Gawain's horse.

ANALYSIS OF MAJOR CHARACTERS

SIR GAWAIN

Though Gawain and Guinevere share the high table at the New Year's celebration in Arthur's court, he describes himself as the least of Arthur's knights in terms of both physical prowess and mental ability. His modest claim to inferiority and his high status at court—he is Arthur's nephew and one of Camelot's most famous knights—testify to both his humility and his ambition. Gawain seeks to improve his inner self throughout the poem. After Gawain arrives at Bertilak's castle in Part 2, it is evident that his reputation is quite widespread. To Gawain, his public reputation is as important as his own opinion of himself, and he therefore insists on wearing the green girdle as a sign of shame at the story's end. He believes that sins should be as visible as virtues.

Even though the Green Knight essentially tricks Gawain by not telling him about his supernatural abilities before asking Gawain to agree to his terms, Gawain refuses to back out of their deal. He stands by his commitments absolutely, even when it means jeopardizing his own life. The poem frequently reiterates Gawain's deep fears and anxieties, but Gawain's desire to maintain his personal integrity at all costs enables him to conquer his fears in his quest for the Green Knight.

Gawain is a paragon of virtue in Parts 1 and 2 of the poem. But in Part 3 he conceals from his host the magical green girdle that the host's wife gives him, revealing that, despite his bravery, Gawain values his own life more than his honesty. Ultimately, however, Gawain confesses his sin to the knight and begs to be pardoned; thereafter, he voluntarily wears the girdle as a symbol of his sin. Because Gawain repents of his sin in such an honorable manner, his one indiscretion in the poem actually ends up being an example of his basic goodness.

Gawain is not a static character. In his encounter with the Green Knight, he recognizes the problematic nature of courtly ideals. When he returns to Arthur's court at Camelot, the other lords and ladies still look to him like lighthearted children, but Gawain is weighed down by a new somberness. Though he survives his quest, Gawain emerges at the end of the poem as a humbled man who realizes his own faults and has to live with the fact that he will never live up to his own high standards.

THE GREEN KNIGHT (ALSO KNOWN AS BERTILAK DE HAUTDESERT AND THE HOST)

The Green Knight is a mysterious, supernatural creature. He rides into Arthur's court on New Year's Eve almost as if summoned by the king's request to hear a marvelous story. His supernatural characteristics, such as his ability to survive decapitation and his green complexion, immediately mark him as a foreboding figure. The Green Knight contrasts with Arthur's court in many ways. The knight symbolizes the wildness, fertility, and death that characterize a primeval world, whereas the court symbolizes an enclave of civilization within the wilderness. But, like the court, the Green Knight strongly advocates the values of the law and justice. And though his long hair suggests an untamed, natural state, his hair is cut into the shape of a courtly garment, suggesting that part of his function is to establish a relationship between wilderness and civilization, past and present.

At Gawain's scheduled beheading, the Green Knight reveals that he is also the host with whom Gawain stayed after his journeys through the wilderness, and that he is known as Bertilak de Hautdesert. As the host, we know Bertilak to be a courteous, jovial man who enjoys hunting for sport and playing games. A well-respected and middle-aged lord, the host contrasts with the beardless Arthur. In fact, his beard is "beaver-hued," a feature which associates the host with the Green Knight. Other clues exist in the text to connect the host with the Green Knight. For instance, both the Green Knight and the host value the power of verbal contracts. Each makes a covenant with Gawain, and the two agreements overlap at the end of the poem.

THEMES, MOTIFS & SYMBOLS

THEMES

THE NATURE OF CHIVALRY

The world of *Sir Gawain and the Green Knight* is governed by well-defined codes of behavior. The code of chivalry, in particular, shapes the values and actions of Sir Gawain and other characters in the poem. The ideals of chivalry derive from the Christian concept of morality, and the proponents of chivalry seek to promote spiritual ideals in a spiritually fallen world.

The ideals of Christian morality and knightly chivalry are brought together in Gawain's symbolic shield. The pentangle represents the five virtues of knights: friendship, generosity, chastity, courtesy, and piety. Gawain's adherence to these virtues is tested throughout the poem, but the poem examines more than Gawain's personal virtue; it asks whether heavenly virtue can operate in a fallen world. What is really being tested in *Sir Gawain and the Green Knight* might be the chivalric system itself, symbolized by Camelot.

Arthur's court depends heavily on the code of chivalry, and *Sir Gawain and the Green Knight* gently criticizes the fact that chivalry values appearance and symbols over truth. Arthur is introduced to us as the "most courteous of all," indicating that people are ranked in this court according to their mastery of a certain code of behavior and good manners. When the Green Knight challenges the court, he mocks them for being so afraid of mere words, suggesting that words and appearances hold too much power over the company. The members of the court never reveal their true feelings, instead choosing to seem beautiful, courteous, and fair-spoken.

On his quest for the Green Chapel, Gawain travels from Camelot into the wilderness. In the forest, Gawain must abandon the codes of chivalry and admit that his animal nature requires him to seek physical comfort in order to survive. Once he prays for help, he is rewarded by the appearance of a castle. The inhabitants of Bertilak's castle teach Gawain about a kind of chivalry that is more firmly based in truth and reality than that of Arthur's court. These people are connected to nature, as their hunting and even the way the servants greet Gawain by kneeling on the "naked earth" symbolize (818). As opposed to the courtiers at Camelot, who celebrate in Part 1 with no understanding of how removed they are from the natural world, Bertilak's courtiers joke self-consciously about how excessively lavish their feast is (889–890).

The poem does not by any means suggest that the codes of chivalry be abandoned. Gawain's adherence to them is what keeps him from sleeping with his host's wife. The lesson Gawain learns as a result of the Green Knight's challenge is that, at a basic level, he is just a physical being who is concerned above all else with his own life. Chivalry provides a valuable set of ideals toward which to strive, but a person must above all remain conscious of his or her own mortality and weakness. Gawain's time in the wilderness, his flinching at the Green Knight's axe, and his acceptance of the lady's offering of the green girdle teach him that though he may be the most chivalrous knight in the land, he is nevertheless human and capable of error.

THE LETTER OF THE LAW

Though the Green Knight refers to his challenge as a "game," he uses the language of the law to bind Gawain into an agreement with him. He repeatedly uses the word "covenant," meaning a set of laws, a word that evokes the two covenants represented by the Old and the New Testaments. The Old Testament details the covenant made between God and the people of Israel through Abraham, but the New Testament replaces the old covenant with a new covenant between Christ and his followers. In 2 Corinthians 3:6, Paul writes that Christ has "a new covenant, not of letter but of spirit; for the letter kills, but the Spirit gives life." The "letter" to which Paul refers here is the legal system of the Old Testament. From this statement comes the Christian belief that the literal enforcement of the law is less important than serving its spirit, a spirit tempered by mercy.

Throughout most of the poem, the covenant between Gawain and the Green Knight evokes the literal kind of legal enforcement that medieval Europeans might have associated with the Old Testament. The Green Knight at first seems concerned solely with the letter of the law. Even though he has tricked Gawain into their covenant, he expects Gawain to follow through on the agreement. And Gawain, though he knows that following the letter of the law means death, is determined to see his agreement through to the end because he sees this as his knightly duty.

At the poem's end, the covenant takes on a new meaning and resembles the less literal, more merciful New Testament covenant between Christ and his Church. In a decidedly Christian gesture, the Green Knight, who is actually Gawain's host, Bertilak, absolves Gawain because Gawain has confessed his faults. To remind Gawain of his weakness, the Green Knight gives him a penance, in the form of the wound on his neck and the girdle. The Green Knight punishes Gawain for breaking his covenant to share all his winnings with his host, but he does not follow to the letter his covenant to decapitate Gawain. Instead of chopping Gawain's head off, Bertilak calls it his right to spare Gawain and only nicks his neck.

Ultimately, Gawain clings to the letter of the law. He cannot accept his sin and absolve himself of it the way Bertilak has, and he continues to do penance by wearing the girdle for the rest of his life. The Green Knight transforms his literal covenant by offering Gawain justice tempered with mercy, but the letter of the law still threatens in the story's background, and in Gawain's own psyche.

MOTIFS

Motifs are recurring structures, contrasts, or literary devices that can help to develop and inform the text's major themes.

THE SEASONS

At the beginning of Parts 2 and 4, the poet describes the changing of the seasons. The seasonal imagery in Part 2 precedes Gawain's departure from Camelot, and in Part 4 his departure from the host's castle. In both cases, the changing seasons correspond to Gawain's changing psychological state, from cheerfulness (pleasant weather) to bleakness (the winter). But the five changing seasons also correspond to the five ages of man (birth/infancy, youth, adulthood, middle age, and old age/death), as well as to the cycles of fertility and decay that govern all creatures in the natural world. The emphasis on the cyclical nature of the seasons contrasts with and provides a different understanding of the passage of time from the more linear narrative of history that frames the poem.

MOTIFS

GAMES

When the poem opens, Arthur's court is engaged in feast-time customs, and Arthur almost seems to elicit the Green Knight's entrance by requesting that someone tell him a tale. When the Green Knight first enters, the courtiers think that his appearance signals a game of some sort. The Green Knight's challenge, the host's later challenge, and the wordplay that takes place between Gawain and the lady are all presented as games. The relationship between games and tests is explored because games are forms of social behavior, while tests provide a measure of an individual's inner worth.

SYMBOLS

Symbols are objects, characters, figures, or colors used to represent abstract ideas or concepts.

THE PENTANGLE

According to the Gawain-poet, King Solomon originally designed the five-pointed star as his own magic seal. A symbol of truth, the star has five points that link and lock with each other, forming what is called the endless knot. Each line of the pentangle passes over one line and under one line, and joins the other two lines at its ends. The pentangle symbolizes the virtues to which Gawain aspires: to be faultless in his five senses; never to fail in his five fingers; to be faithful to the five wounds that Christ received on the cross; to be strengthened by the five joys that the Virgin Mary had in Jesus (the Annunciation, Nativity, Resurrection, Ascension, and Assumption); and to possess brotherly love, courtesy, piety, and chastity. The side of the shield facing Gawain contains an image of the Virgin Mary to make sure that Gawain never loses heart.

THE GREEN GIRDLE

The meaning of the host's wife's girdle changes over the course of the narrative. It is made out of green silk and embroidered with gold thread, colors that link it to the Green Knight. She claims it possesses the power to keep its wearer from harm, but we find out in Part 4 that the girdle has no magical properties. After the Green Knight reveals his identity as the host, Gawain curses the girdle as representing cowardice and an excessive love of mortal life. He wears it from then on as a badge of his sinfulness. To show their support, Arthur and his followers wear green silk baldrics that look just like Gawain's girdle.

SUMMARY & ANALYSIS

PART 1 (LINES 1–490)

> *Great wonder grew in hall*
> *At his hue most strange to see,*
> *For man and gear and all*
> *Were green as green could be.*
>
> (See QUOTATIONS, p. 33)

SUMMARY

The poem opens with a mythological account of Britain's founding. After the fall of Troy, we are told, various heroes left to build cities. Romulus founded Rome, Ticius founded Tuscany, and Brutus founded Britain. The author introduces Britain's greatest leader, the legendary King Arthur. This brief introduction ends with the poet telling us he will relate a story he heard told in a hall about a great Arthurian adventure.

The story begins at Christmastime at King Arthur's court in Camelot. The knights of the Round Table join Arthur in the holiday celebrations, and Queen Guinevere presides in their midst. The lords and ladies of Camelot have been feasting for fifteen days, and now it is New Year's Day. Everyone participates in New Year's games, exchanging gifts and kisses. When the evening's feast is about to be served, Arthur introduces a new game: he refuses to eat his dinner until he has heard a marvelous story.

While the lords and ladies feast, with Arthur's nephew Gawain and Guinevere sitting together in the place of privilege at the high table, Arthur continues to wait for his marvel. As if in answer to Arthur's request, an unknown knight suddenly enters the hall on horseback. The gigantic knight has a beautiful face and figure. Every piece of his elaborate costume is green, with flourishes of gold embossing. His huge horse is green, and his green hair and beard are woven together with gold thread. He holds a holly bob in one hand and a huge green and gold axe in the other.

Without introducing himself, the knight demands to see the person in charge. His question meets dead silence—the stunned lords and ladies stare at him silently, waiting for Arthur to respond.

Arthur steps forward, inviting the knight to join the feast and tell his tale after he has dismounted from his horse. The knight refuses the invitation, remaining mounted and explaining that he has come to inspect Arthur's court because he has heard so much about its superior knights. He claims to come in peace, but he demands to be indulged in a game. Arthur assumes the knight refers to some kind of combat and promises him a fight. However, the knight explains that he has no interest in fighting with such young and puny knights. Instead, he wants to play a game in which someone will strike him with his own axe, on the understanding that he gets to return the blow in exactly a year and a day.

The strange conditions of the game shock the court into silence once again. The Green Knight begins to question the reputation of Arthur's followers, claiming that their failure to respond proves them cowards. Arthur blushes and steps forth defend his court, but just as he begins to swing the giant axe at the unfazed Green Knight, Gawain stands up and requests that he be allowed to take the challenge himself. The king agrees, and Gawain recites the terms of the game to show the Green Knight that he understands the pact he has undertaken. The Green Knight dismounts and bends down toward the ground, exposing his neck. Gawain lifts the axe, and in one stroke he severs the Green Knight's head. Blood spurts from the wound, and the head rolls around the room, passing by the feet of many of the guests. However, the Green Knight does not fall from his horse. He reaches down, picks up the head, and holds it before him, pointing it toward the high table. The head speaks, reiterating the terms of Gawain's promise. The Green Knight rides out of the hall, sparks flying from his horse's hooves. Arthur and Gawain decide to hang the axe above the main dais. They then return to their feast and the continuing festivities.

ANALYSIS

By framing the central plot of *Sir Gawain and the Green Knight* with an account of Britain's founding by the Trojan Brutus, the poet establishes Camelot's political legitimacy. He also links his own story with classical epics such as Virgil's *Aeneid*, thereby creating a literary connection to the ancient world. In the second stanza, the poet claims that he heard the original story of Sir Gawain recited "in hall" (3 1), but also that it was "linked in measures meetly / By letters tried and true" (that is, it appeared in written format) (3 5–3 6). Iin addition to giving his poem both political and literary roots, the poet gives his poem both an oral and a written history, all in two brief stanzas.

The author devotes a lot of space to describing the lavish, intricate details of the feast, including the guests, their clothing, and the hall itself. The knights and ladies of Arthur's court are full of vitality and joy, resembling the New Year that they celebrate. The poet describes them as "fair folk in their first age," and he uses words like fresh, lovely, comely, young, and mirthful to describe them (54). Later, the Green Knight echoes these descriptions but exaggerates them, calling Arthur and his knights "beardless children" (280). These descriptions of Arthur's courtiers as children in their "first age" implicitly compare the court to humankind in its "first age," before the Fall in the Garden of Eden. The emphasis on the court's youth and lack of experience suggests that these youthful people might be capable of failure, error, bad judgment, and sinfulness, just as Adam and Eve were.

The poet's description of Queen Guinevere sitting on her dais, surrounded by exotic tapestries and jewels, suggests that the queen herself is first and foremost a beautiful object. The fact that Guinevere sits surrounded by tapestries from the far reaches of the earth supports the poet's hyperbolic insistence that Guinevere's beauty surpasses that of all women in the world. The poet does not touch on the moral or ethical aspects of Guinevere's character—whether her exceptional body hides an ugly soul or enshrines a pure one remains for the reader to decide. However, any medieval reader would recognize Guinevere's youthful beauty as the very thing that will later bring about the fall of Camelot: she is destined to betray her husband with Lancelot.

The Green Knight provides a less ambivalent commentary on Arthur and his courtiers by branding them inexperienced children in need of testing. At the same time, the Green Knight's own character remains ambiguous, so we don't know whether or not we can trust his judgment. The knight's green costume and the holly bob he holds in one hand symbolize nature and fertility, but his costume is also ornamented with gold and he carries an axe, symbols of artifice and civilization. The Green Knight represents both the artificial and the natural worlds, and he seems to be a superhuman as well as a supernatural figure. These implications are confirmed when the Green Knight survives decapitation, showing himself to have the power of resurrection.

Gawain's placement at the high table and his blood ties with Arthur characterize him as someone who maintains a high status among the knights of the Round Table. Yet, when Gawain steps forth to accept the Green Knight's challenge, he claims he is the weakest of Arthur's knights. Again, the author refuses to indicate whether Gawain's self-deprecation stems from a real sense of his own inadequacy or whether it hides a kind of boastful knowledge of his own knightly stature. Many scholars of medieval chivalry believe Gawain's behavior in this scene accords with the rules of knightly courtesy, but the poem gives us no commentary on Gawain's motivations at this crucial plot juncture.

Although the Green Knight refers to his agreement with Gawain as a "game," suggesting that the challenge is no different from any of the other games played by Arthur's court, the Green Knight words his challenge like a legal contract. He refers to the agreement as a "covenant" and mentions dues, and he makes Gawain repeat the terms multiple times. The Green Knight's language foreshadows the fact that the his game will have serious ethical implications; it will test not only Gawain's bravery, but also his honesty and integrity.

PART 2 (LINES 491–1125)

> *A year passes apace, and proves ever new:*
> *First things and final conform but seldom.*
>
> (See QUOTATIONS, p. 34)

SUMMARY

Part 2 begins with a brief summary of the New Year's feast in Part 1. The poet calls the Green Knight's game with Gawain King Arthur's New Year's gift, since it provided him with the marvelous story he had waited to hear. The poet describes in elaborate language the change of seasons, from Christmas to the cold season of Lent with its ritual fasting, to a green young spring and summer, then into harvest time, and finally back to winter. In late autumn, on the Day of All Saints, the knights of Camelot prepare to send a mournful Gawain off on his quest for the Green Chapel.

Worried but resigned, Gawain calls for his armor, which the poet describes in great detail. He devotes space to each and every piece, down to the shimmering skirts on Gawain's horse, Gringolet. The description lingers on Gawain's shield, which depicts on its outside a gold five-pointed star, or pentangle, on a red background. On the inside of the shield is the face of Mary, Christ's mother. Each of the five points of the pentangle, which is described as an "endless knot" (630), represents a set of Gawain's virtues: his five senses; his five fingers; his fidelity, founded on the five wounds of Christ; his force, founded on the five joys of Mary; and the five knightly virtues.

After dressing, Gawain says goodbye to his friends and leaves the court. Sparks fly from Gringolet's hooves as they ride off. He heads out into the wilderness, traveling through North Wales and the west coast of England in his search for the mysterious Green Chapel. He encounters various foes—wolves and dragons, bulls and bears, boars and giants—but always prevails over his enemies. He sleeps in his armor and has frequent nightmares. As the winter grows colder, he nearly freezes to death.

Finally, on Christmas Eve, the desperate Gawain prays to the Virgin Mary that he might find a place to attend Christmas Mass. He repents his sins, crosses himself three times, and, when he looks up, he sees a beautiful castle. Surrounded by a green park and a moat, the castle shimmers in the distance through the trees, and Gawain, full of thanks to God for saving him, approaches the drawbridge. The castle is so white and its crowns and turrets so tall and intricately carved that the whole building looks as if it were cut out of paper. Gawain salutes, and a guardian allows him to enter.

The porter welcomes Gawain warmly, inviting him in to meet the courtiers and the lord of the castle. The host's lords and ladies repeatedly express their joy that Gawain (a minor celebrity because he is Arthur's nephew and a knight of the Round Table) can show them the latest in knightly behavior and help them to become more courtly themselves. Like Arthur's followers, the courtiers seem inexperienced and carefree. But Gawain's host presents a much more imposing figure than Arthur. The lord appears to be middle-aged, with a thick, gray-black beard and solid, sturdy legs. Though the host's fiery face and stocky figure make him appear fierce, his speech reveals him to be gracious and gentle.

The lord takes Gawain to a rich chamber, where he feeds Gawain sumptuous food and wine, and introduces Gawain to two women. The host's wife is young, beautiful, and elegantly dressed, her firm neck and bosom exposed. The other, an old woman, is wrinkled, stocky, hairy, black-browed, and covered entirely in clothing. Only her nose, eyes, and blistered lips are exposed by the fabric. After the introductions, the lords and ladies play games and celebrate late into the night, when Gawain retires for bed.

Christmas morning and the two days following it pass in a similar manner, but Gawain begins to feel the weight of his quest pressing on him. With only three days remaining before his engagement with the Green Knight, Gawain refuses his host's offer of a longer stay, explaining that he must search for the Green Chapel or else be judged a failure. The host responds gleefully, telling Gawain he can send him to the Green Chapel easily—it is only two miles away. Gladdened, Gawain thanks the host and accepts the invitation to stay the three days until New Year's. The host proposes a game of sorts: during the day, he wants Gawain to stay at court and linger in bed and around the castle, spending time with the two ladies. Meanwhile, the host will go out hunting with his men. At the end of each of the three days, the two men will exchange whatever they have won. Happy to play along, Gawain accepts. The men kiss each other, repeating their vows, and then go off to bed.

> The good knight on Gringolet thought it great luck
> If he could but contrive to come there within
> To keep the Christmas feast in that castle fair and bright.
> (See QUOTATIONS, p. 35)

ANALYSIS

The opening lines of Part 2, which detail the changing seasons of the year, seem a digression from the tale, but they actually correlate very closely with Gawain's changing state of mind. Just as the external world shifts over the course of a year, so too does Gawain's inner climate. He transforms from a joyous youth to a mournful figure as the world passes from winter to summer and back again. The seasonal imagery sets a tone of mutability and instability for the rest of the story, which is important because Gawain is soon called upon to demonstrate steadfastness in a world that is designed to change and be changed by the cycles of life and death.

When Gawain's prayer brings into being a castle that didn't exist moments before, it seems as if Gawain's senses falter, as he sees what looks very much like a mirage glimmering in the distance. The five senses are one of the five virtues represented by the pentangle on Gawain's shield, and during his stay at the host's castle, each of the qualities represented by five points of the pentangle will fail Gawain.

Once inside its walls, Gawain's physical abilities (his five senses and his five fingers) fail him again, beginning when the "wine goes to his head" at line 900 and continuing as he proceeds to spend all of his time lounging around the castle. Further, although Gawain frequently calls on Jesus and Mary for aid in the wilderness, once inside the court, his piety fades to the background, and his devotion to the five wounds of Christ and five joys of Mary cease to function as defenses. With his physical and spiritual defenses faltering, Gawain's five knightly virtues—friendship, generosity, courtesy, chastity, and piety—undergo examination by his host in Parts 3 and 4.

Though the mysterious court seems beautiful and safe, the poet's descriptions of the castle and its inhabitants give us many clues that it holds deep dangers for Gawain. Along with Gawain, we learn not to trust physical appearances, because Gawain's perceptions prove unreliable and the things he perceives unstable. The miragelike way in which the host's castle appears to Gawain foreshadows that things are not as they seem—if one mirage can deceive Gawain's senses, others can as well. Also, the host's physique and his initiation of a covenant, disguised as a harmless game, recall the character of the Green Knight from Part 1. Though the host's proposed game seems innocent enough, he makes Gawain repeat the terms of the agreement, just as the Green Knight did at Camelot.

The poet describes the two women as "unlike to look upon . . . / For if the one was fresh, the other was faded" (950–951). The poet's language suggests that although the two women may be "unlike to look upon," they are not completely unlike in other ways. By describing the younger woman as "fresh" and the older woman as "faded," the poet suggests that the two women form two ends of the same spectrum. The old woman functions as a memento mori (a Latin phrase meaning "remember death"), who reminds the reader of the unavoidable destruction of the physical world. Furthermore, in medieval iconography, an old woman next to a young woman often allegorically represents vanity. The significance of such a representation was that love of worldly beauty means neglect of the spiritual life, and since worldly beauty must always fail and die, its pursuit will always prove vain.

PART 3 (LINES 1126–1997)

Sir, if you be Gawain, it seems a great wonder—
A man so well-meaning, and mannerly disposed,
And cannot act in company as courtesy bids,

(See QUOTATIONS, p. 36)

SUMMARY

Early in the morning, the host and his guests get out of bed and prepare to ride forth from the castle. They attend Mass, eat a small breakfast, and leave with their hunting dogs as dawn breaks. They ride through the woods, chasing after the deer and herding the does away from the bucks and harts. In the fields, they slay the deer dozens at a time with their deadly arrows. The hounds hunt down the wounded animals, and the hunters follow to kill them off with their knives.

Back at the castle, Gawain lingers in bed until daybreak. While still half asleep, he hears the door open quietly. Peeking out of his bed's canopy, he sees the host's wife creeping toward his bed. Gawain lies back down, pretending to be asleep. Stealthily, the lady climbs inside the bed curtains and sits beside Gawain. Confused but curious, Gawain stretches and pretends to wake up. Upon seeing the lady in his bed, he feigns surprise and makes the sign of the cross. The host's wife smiles and greets him, teasing him for sleeping so deeply that he didn't notice her entering his chamber. She jokes that she has captured him, and she threatens to tie him to the bed, laughing at her own game. Gawain laughs and "surrenders" to her, then asks her leave to get up and put on his clothes. She refuses, saying that instead she will hold him captive. She tells Gawain that she has heard many stories about him and wants to spend time alone with him. She offers to be his servant and tells him to use her body any way he sees fit.

The two continue bantering, and the lady tells Gawain that she would have chosen him for her husband if she could have. Gawain responds that her own husband is the better man. Until mid-morning, the lady continues to lavish Gawain with admiration, and Gawain continues to guard himself while still being gracious.

When the lady gets up to leave, she laughs and then sternly accuses her captive knight of not being the real Gawain. Alarmed and worried that he has failed in his courtesy, Gawain asks her to explain what she means. She responds that the real Gawain would never let a lady leave his chamber without taking a kiss. Gawain allows one kiss, and then the lady leaves. He dresses immediately and goes to hear Mass, then spends the afternoon with the host's wife and the old woman.

Meanwhile, the lord has been hunting deer with his men all day. As evening comes on, the hunters begin to flay the animals, separating the meat and skin from the carcasses. The poet describes the dismembering of the deer in gory detail, from the removal of their bowels to the severing of their heads. After they finish their bloody task, the hunters return home with their meat.

The host greets Gawain and gives him the venison he won during the hunt that day. Gawain thanks him and in return gives him the kiss he won from the lady. The host jokingly asks where Gawain won such a prize, and Gawain points out that they agreed to exchange winnings, not to tell where or how they were acquired. Happy, the men feast and retire to bed, agreeing before they part to play the game again the next day.

The next two days follow a similar pattern. On the second day, the lord hunts a wild boar, risking his life as he wrestles it to the ground and stabs it with his sword. At the castle, the lady continues to teasingly challenge Gawain's reputation, pressuring him into allowing her two kisses and continuing to make convincing arguments for how his acceptance of her love would be chivalrous. That night, the host brings home the boar's head on a stick and exchanges it with Gawain for the two kisses.

On the third day the host hunts a fox, and Gawain, awakened by the lady from horrible nightmares about the Green Knight, receives three kisses from the lady during the course of their conversation. However, while they banter, the lady asks Gawain for a love token. Gawain refuses to fulfill her request, claiming he has nothing to give, so the lady offers him a ring, which he also refuses. She then offers him her green girdle, which she claims has magical properties: it possesses the ability to keep the man who wears it safe from death. Tempted by the possibility of protecting his life, Gawain accepts the girdle.

That afternoon, Gawain goes to confession. At the end of the day, he gives the three kisses to his host but fails to mention the lady's gift. After the exchange, the host and his courtiers hold a farewell party for Gawain, who later retires to his chamber, prepared to leave the next day to seek out the Green Chapel. Whether he sleeps or not, the poet cannot say.

ANALYSIS

The alternating hunting scenes and bedroom scenes narrated in Part 3 parallel one another, suggesting an analogous relationship between the lady's attempts to entrap Gawain and the lord's attempts to catch his prey. Each of the three days begins and ends with the violent, fast-paced action of the chase, and embedded at the center of each day is the courtly, bawdy bedroom scene. For both the hunters and Gawain, each day leads to a more valuable—and more dangerous—set of winnings. The three hunting scenes portray the larger patterns of the poem in brief allegories. The hunting scenes and the seduction scenes together address all the major issues of the poem.

There are a number of parallels between the hunt scenes and Gawain's own quest. The host considers his gory and dangerous hunts "sport" in the same way the Green Knight considers his pact with Gawain a "game," and, like the Green Knight's challenge, the hunt scenes test the hunters' nobility. The way the doe hunt starts out by separating the victims from the herd brings to mind the Green Knight's challenge to Arthur and his company. The deer hunt happens at a group level, with multiple hunters and the mass execution of dozens of animals. In medieval hunting guides and bestiaries, deer are ranked as "beasts of venery" or "beasts of chase." Though not fierce or confrontational, the animals were considered noble to hunt because they challenged their hunters' skill and because their meat and hides have use value.

The boar hunt, on the other hand, engages the host and his prey in one-on-one combat. Boars were also considered beasts of venery, but were among the most dangerous game when cornered. That the host decapitates the boar and carries his head into the castle on a pike also recalls Gawain's imminent decapitation. Interestingly, the foxes hunted on the third and final hunt were, in the Middle Ages, considered mere rodents, of the lowest class of the beasts of venery. Though difficult to hunt, they represented no real nobility or value, and were considered ignoble and deceitful animals whose fur possessed little usefulness or beauty. Thus, to spend the entire day hunting and to bring back nothing but what the host calls a "foul fox pelt" seems like time and energy wasted (1944). On this third day, we might expect the prize to have more value, but the host's winnings have no worth at all, a fact he points out to Gawain during the exchange.

The three bedroom scenes also take the form of games, and they also build toward an anticlimax. The lady plays a new kind of game with Gawain, putting him in a precarious situation by testing two knightly virtues that she places at odds with one another: his courtesy and chastity. When Gawain refuses to give in to the lady sexually, she accuses him of being discourteous; as soon as he responds in a more courteous manner, the lady again pushes him toward being unchaste. The lady's arguments, which are duplicitous and highly persuasive, vary between complex subtlety and bawdy suggestion. During their first bedroom encounter she claims innocently that she wants to "pass an hour in pastime with pleasant words" (1253), and she seems pious when she praises God for putting in her hands "all hearts' desire" (1257). Yet we know that she is pinning a naked Gawain to the bed, holding him in her arms.

By claiming that she possesses Gawain only through God's grace, the lady evokes a complicated system of religious and political imagery. As the host's wife and as a noblewoman more generally, the lady exceeds Gawain in rank, and his chivalry requires him to obey her, facts of which she reminds him when attempting to seduce him. Also, the notion that courtly love—the love a knight might have for a lady of higher rank than himself—leads to spiritual ennoblement had been popularized centuries earlier in continental literature. Invoking religion at this erotically charged moment reminds Gawain that part of his spiritual education as a knight should involve courtly love. For Gawain to refuse her advances, he must break his knightly responsibility to be courteous; for him to accept, he must break his chastity.

On the third day, Gawain's resolve weakens when the stakes shift radically from courtesy versus chastity to honesty versus safety. On the surface, the green silk girdle that the lady offers Gawain looks exactly like the kind of token that a courtly lady might give her lover (and Gawain initially rejects it for this reason), yet the ethical dilemma it represents is related to self-preservation rather than to chastity. When the lady tells him that the girdle also protects its wearer from being wounded or killed, Gawain is eager to be able to fulfill his promise to the Green Knight and still survive. What Gawain wants is a loophole through which he can escape death but still honor his covenant with the Green Knight. Unfortunately, using this loophole requires him to deceive his host—a breach of honesty and gratitude for hospitality. Gawain does not notice that the girdle's silk is green and gold, like the Green Knight's clothing, and he disassociates the girdle itself from the lady's body, which it surely symbolizes, despite its magical properties, or else accepting it would not have been taboo in the first place.

Though in the end Gawain does not sleep with the host's wife, and though he does not view lying about the magical girdle to save his life to be as big a crime as adultery, the omission nevertheless breaks his vow with the host. In desiring to find a loophole in his covenant with the Green Knight, Gawain also seeks to create one in his agreement with the host. The fact that Gawain goes to confess his sins immediately after taking the girdle indicates that he knows he has broken his vow.

One medieval scholar famously asked what Gawain would have to give the host if he had in fact slept with the lady, and the possibility of Gawain and the host's wife having sex certainly raises this question. Consequently, homoeroticism is at the heart of the exchange-of-winnings game, since Gawain's winnings are inevitably in the form of sexual favors, and since he is required by his pact with the host to give his winnings to the host at the end of the day. The logical outcome, if the lady had succeeded, would be that Gawain and the host would have to sleep together. The erotic scenario in *Sir Gawain and the Green Knight* creates a triangulation of desire: through their mutual attentions to the host's wife, Gawain and the host establish an implicitly sexual connection with one another.

PART 4 (LINES 1998–2531)

SUMMARY

Gawain lies in bed during the early hours of New Year's morning, listening to the harsh wind wailing outside the castle. Before the sun comes up, he rises and prepares to depart, putting on his armor and ordering servants to saddle his horse. Despite Gawain's anxiety, his armor shines as brightly as it did when he left Camelot. He does not forget to tie the lady's girdle around his waist. The girdle's green color stands out against the red cloth of Gawain's surcoat.

As Gawain and Gringolet prepare to ride off, Gawain silently blesses the castle, asking Christ to keep it safe from harm and wishing joy on the host and the host's wife. Accompanied by a guide, Gawain crosses the drawbridge and rides back out into the wilderness, up to the heights of the neighboring snowy hills. There, the guide turns to Gawain and proposes a solution to his impending problem: if Gawain leaves now without facing the knight, the guide promises not to tell anyone. No one survives an encounter with the Green Knight, the guide informs Gawain, so continuing is tantamount to suicide. Gawain thanks the guide for his concern, but he refuses to be a coward. The guide wishes Gawain well and leaves at a breakneck pace, afraid to go any farther into the woods.

Gawain strengthens his resolve and heads onward into the strange forest. He sees no sign of buildings and searches without success for a chapel in the wilderness. Finally he notices a strange mound and investigates it. He spots a kind of crevice or cave, fringed with tall grass, and realizes it must be the Green Chapel.

Suddenly certain that the place belongs to the devil, Gawain curses the chapel and is proceeding toward the cave with his lance in hand when he hears the horrifying sound of a weapon being sharpened on a grindstone. Terrified, and fully aware that the sound means his own doom, Gawain calls out to the lord of the place, stating that he has come to fulfill his agreement. The Green Knight replies, telling Gawain to stay put, and continues to sharpen his weapon. The Green Knight emerges from around a crag, carrying a Danish axe. He welcomes Gawain warmly and compliments him on his punctuality, then tells him he will repay him for his own beheading a year ago. Gawain tries to act unafraid as he bares his neck for the deadly blow.

The Green Knight lifts the axe high and drops it. When the Green Knight sees Gawain flinch he stops his blade, mocking Gawain and questioning his reputation. Gawain tells him he will not flinch again, and the Green Knight lifts the axe a second time. Gawain doesn't flinch as the axe comes down, and the Green Knight holds the blade again, this time congratulating Gawain's courage. He then threatens Gawain, saying that the next blow will strike him. Angry, Gawain tells the knight to hurry up and strike, and the knight lifts his axe one last time. He brings it down hard, but causes Gawain no harm other than a slight cut on his neck. Gawain leaps away, draws his sword gleefully, and challenges the Green Knight to a fight, telling him that he has withstood the promised blow. The Green Knight leans on his axe and agrees that Gawain has met the terms of the covenant, but refuses to fight. He points out that he has spared Gawain. He feinted the first two times, in accordance with their contract on the first two days, when Gawain gave him the gifts he had received from the lady. The nick from the third blow was punishment for Gawain's behavior on the third day, when he failed to tell the truth about the green girdle.

This speech reveals that the Green Knight is the host of the castle where Gawain was staying. He again congratulates Gawain on his bravery, calling him the worthiest of Arthur's knights and excusing his transgression on the third day. Gawain responds by untying the girdle and cursing it, and asking to regain the host's trust if possible. The Green Knight laughs and absolves Gawain, now that he has adequately confessed his sin. He gives Gawain the girdle to keep and asks him to come back to the castle and stay there longer to celebrate New Year's, but Gawain refuses.

Gawain thanks the Green Knight and sends his best wishes to the lady and the old woman, then complains about the deceitfulness of women, who have brought about the downfalls of great men such as Adam, Solomon, Samson, and David. He accepts the girdle, though, and asks that the Green Knight tell him his true name. The knight agrees and reveals himself as Bertilak de Hautdesert, servant of Morgan le Faye, who is the old woman in the castle. Le Faye is also Gawain's aunt and Arthur's half sister, as well as Merlin's mistress; she sometimes helps and sometimes makes trouble for Arthur. Bertilak reveals that Le Faye sent him in disguise as the Green Knight to Camelot in order to scare Queen Guinevere to death. One last time, Bertilak asks Gawain to return with him to the castle and celebrate New Year's with Morgan le Faye and the others, but Gawain refuses and hurries back toward Camelot.

On his journey back to Arthur's castle, Gawain's wound heals, but he continues to wear the green girdle on his right shoulder. When he enters the court, he meets a gleeful reception and tells the story of his encounter with Bertilak. He explains that he intends to wear the green girdle forever as a sign of his failure and sin. Arthur and the court try to comfort Gawain, and they decide that they will all wear belts of green silk as a sign of respect and unity.

The poet concludes by reaffirming the truth of his story, which happened in the days of King Arthur, and which is recorded in "[t]he books of Brutus' deeds" (2523). In the last wheel of the poem, the poet praises Christ.

And one and all fell prey
To women they had used;
If I be led astray,
Methinks I may be excused.

(See QUOTATIONS, p. 37)

ANALYSIS

Echoing the opening of Part 2, Part 4 opens with a description of the passing of time and a general description of the atmosphere, followed by an account of Gawain putting on his armor and leaving the castle. Though briefer and more somber in tone, this second description balances the earlier one and begins to bring the poem toward its close. The harshness of the winter, with its howling wind and numbing cold, fits Gawain's bleak mood.

The date on which Gawain sets out to find the Green Chapel is important. In the medieval liturgical calendar, January first marked the Feast of the Circumcision. (In the Judaic tradition, circumcision took place exactly eight days after a child's birth, so Christ's circumcision occurred on January 1, eight days after December 25.) The Green Knight's beheading occurred a year and a day earlier, on the eve of the Feast of the Circumcision, suggesting a parallel between the Green Knight's head and the foreskin of Christ. That the Green Knight is able to reassemble himself after his decapitation recalls Christian belief in Christ's resurrection and in the resurrection of all bodies after Judgment Day. On the New Year's Day a year and a day after the Green Knight's symbolic circumcision, the Green Knight punishes Gawain not by decapitating him, but by lightly cutting his neck. This cut symbolizes circumcision as well, but it lacks the supernatural elements of the Green Knight's punishment.

The axe that the Green Knight is sharpening when Gawain finds him is evidence of the knight's contrast to the courtly tradition from which Gawain comes. At Camelot, the knight's axe is described at length, and in the forest, we discover that the Green Knight possesses a new Danish axe that replaces the one Gawain and Arthur hung up in the hall at Camelot. The Danish axe connects the Green Knight with England's Anglo-Saxon roots. Originally associated with the Vikings, the presence of the Danish war axe aligns the Green Knight with a regime that is older than the one Gawain's lance represents. As such, the Green Knight represents a relationship with a primeval human existence.

When the Green Knight spares Gawain, it is clear that the knight has changed from a character obsessed with the absolute justice of pacts and agreements into one who understands the possibility of compassion and mercy. Up until this part, the Green Knight has seemed to privilege the exact letter of his covenant with Gawain above mercy or even justice. But at the end of the story, he transforms into a much more compassionate figure. He calls it his right to spare Gawain from decapitation, and explains, "You are so fully confessed, your failings made known, / And bear the plain penance at the point of my blade" (2391–2392). The combination of an Old Testament rite, the circumcision, with a New Testament one, the confession, frees Gawain from the sin of lying about the girdle.

Important Quotations Explained

1.   There hurtles in at the hall-door an unknown rider,
One the greatest on ground in growth of his frame:
From broad neck to buttocks so bulky and thick,
And his loins and his legs so long and so great,
Half a giant on earth I hold him to be,
But believe him no less than the largest of men,
And the seemliest in his stature to see, as he rides,
For in back and in breast though his body was grim,
His waist in its width was worthily small,
And formed with every feature in fair accord
                    was he.
          Great wonder grew in hall
          At his hue most strange to see,
          For man and gear and all
          Were green as green could be.
                  (136–150)

This quotation from Part 1 describes the Green Knight's first appearance in Arthur's court, and it serves as our introduction to the mysterious character as well. The Gawain-poet's description employs hyperbole, as in the superlatives "greatest," "largest," and "seemliest." The poet's repetition of the word "so," and his insistence that the knight stretches the limits of ordinary reality—he is "[h]alf a giant on earth"—reinforce this hyperbole and contribute to our sense that the Green Knight is larger than life. The poet's comparison of the Green Knight to a half-giant may be an allusion to a passage in Genesis just before the story of Noah that claims that fallen angels and human women mated together to produce super-human, wicked children, precipitating God's punishment in the form of the flood (Gen. 6:1–4).

After claiming that the Green Knight looks like a giant, the poet goes on to reassure his audience that the Green Knight is in fact a human being, even an extremely good-looking one. With fair fea-tures and a form composed of clean lines (broad shoulders tapering into a thin waist), the Green Knight cuts a beautiful figure. The description builds up to the bob—"was he"—with increasing suspense, and not until the wheel do we learn that the beautiful knight is green. In this passage, the poet uses the bob and wheel as a tension-creating device, snaking us through a lengthy description before we get to the important revelation of the knight's green color in the last quatrain. This style also lends a sense of foreboding to the Green Knight, who looks almost human, but whose gigantic stature and green complexion seem to associate him with the supernatural—and, worse still, with some kind of primitive evil.

2.   Gawain was glad to begin those games in hall,
      But if the end be harsher, hold it no wonder,
      For though men are merry in mind after much drink,
      A year passes apace, and proves ever new:
      First things and final conform but seldom.

                                    (495–499)

This passage from the beginning of Part 2 describes the passage of time, a phenomenon that the poet exploits to highlight the necessary mutability of the natural world, including mankind. No matter what any man does, he will be touched and changed over time. The poem opposes the circular nature of a year, which "proves ever new," to the linear nature of human experience, which in Gawain's case changes from merriment to harsh conditions in the span of a year. The extremity of these two conditions brings to mind the inevitability that individuals will be affected by forces outside themselves.

The Gawain-poet warns his readers not to be surprised if his story ends unhappily. He suggests that the way to deal with the inevitable shifts in their fortunes is to maintain a light approach to life. In the original language, the author employs a metaphor in the last line that gets lost in translation. A more literal translation of that line is "the beginning and the end fold together but seldom." This metaphor compares life to a string or a piece of fabric that doesn't fold together evenly and neatly, recalling the Fates of classical mythology, who measure out man's life with thread. It also highlights one of the poem's central concerns, the relationship among birth, death, and rebirth.

3. [T]here hoved a great hall and fair:
    Turrets rising in tiers, with tines at their tops,
    Spires set beside them, splendidly long,
    With finials well-fashioned, as filigree fine.
    Chalk-white chimneys over chambers high
    Gleamed in gay array upon gables and roofs;
    The pinnacles in panoply, pointing in air,
    So vied there for his view that verily it seemed
    A castle cut of paper for a king's feast.
    The good knight on Gringolet thought it great luck
    If he could but contrive to come there within
    To keep the Christmas feast in that castle fair
                              and bright.
                    (794–806)

This passage describes Gawain's first sighting of the host's castle, in Part 2 of the poem. Starving and freezing, Gawain prays to Mary to find a place where he can celebrate Christmas Mass, then looks up suddenly to notice a building he hadn't seen before. The Gawain-poet describes the building as a kind of fairy castle, with countless, skillfully crafted towers and spires, all gleaming white. In this passage, the poet gives us a number of clues about the true nature of the castle and foreshadows the revelation at the end of the poem that the host and the Green Knight are the same person.

At this point in the poem, Gawain begins to look very much like a pilgrim. He wanders through the wilderness praying and fasting, looking for a sacred place. What he finds is the host's castle, whose incredible beauty represents a holy answer to his prayer. To Gawain, the castle looks "grand and fine," and to a medieval Christian reader, it might sound very much like the legendary New Jerusalem of Revelations. In the Christian tradition, the physical pilgrimage to Jerusalem provides an allegory for the spiritual pilgrimage of the human soul to heaven. Here, the fantastically pure towers might at first blush seem to evoke the holy city. However, the poet tells us the castle also looks as though it were cut out of cardboard or paper. Though it appears to be a safe haven, and even like the heavenly city to which all Christian souls should aspire, the poet lets the reader know that this castle is a mere facade. Gawain does not realize his mistake until Part 4.

4.   "Sir, if you be Gawain, it seems a great wonder—
       A man so well-meaning, and mannerly disposed,
       And cannot act in company as courtesy bids,
       And if one takes the trouble to teach him, 'tis all in vain.
       That lesson learned lately is lightly forgot,
       Though I painted it as plain as my poor wit allowed."
       "What lesson, dear lady?" he asked all alarmed;
       "I have been much to blame, if your story be true."
       "Yet my counsel was of kissing," came her answer then,
       "Where favor has been found, freely to claim
       As accords with the conduct of courteous knights."
                                        (1481–1491)

In Part 3, Gawain and the host's wife have this exchange on the second morning of Gawain's game with the host. The lady's comments
highlight the tension between courtesy and chastity, a tension she
exploits in an attempt to get what she wants. The lady starts out by
challenging Gawain's name and reputation, claiming that her guest
cannot be the real Gawain, because that famous knight would not
forget to be "gracious." She likens him to an errant student who has
forgotten his lesson from the day before and herself to his teacher. In
doing so, she calls upon a huge store of cultural imagery from the
courtly love and classical traditions.

    In the courtly love tradition, the beloved lady ideally works as a
kind of erotic teacher, instructing the lover in proper spiritual com-
portment as well as in the courtly "art of love." The courtly lady is
supposed to ennoble her knight by teaching him how to be a proper
lover and a better man. At the same time, the host's wife evokes the
classical tradition of education, in which female allegorical figures
such as Lady Grammar and Lady Philosophy are responsible for the
education of boys and men. Not only does the lady construct herself
as Gawain's sexual teacher, but she also imagines herself as his
schoolmistress in the arts of speaking and behaving properly. The
courtly and the classical traditions are by no means mutually exclu-
sive, but their cooperation here lends force to the lady's attempts to
persuade Gawain to give up his chastity, as Gawain's troubled
response attests.

5.   But if a dullard should dote, deem it no wonder,
And through the wiles of a woman be wooed into sorrow,
For so was Adam by one, when the world began,
And Solomon by many more, and Samson the mighty—
Delilah was his doom, and David thereafter
Was beguiled by Bathsheba, and bore much distress;

. . . .

For these were proud princes, most prosperous of old,
Past all lovers lucky, that languished under heaven,
                bemused.
        And one and all fell prey
        To women they had used;
        If I be led astry,
        Methinks I may be excused.
          (2414–2419, 2422–2428)

In this quotation from the end of the poem, Gawain compares himself to famous biblical figures who were led astray by the deceitful tricks of women. However, the examples Gawain names are increasingly dissimilar to him, so that each example weakens his argument further until it falls apart completely when he compares himself to David. Eve beguiled Adam into eating from the Tree of Life in a way similar to the way the host's wife beguiles Gawain, but the serpent had already beguiled Eve, which partly excuses her action—just as Morgan le Faye charmed the host and his lady. Delilah tricked Samson, but she did so on behalf of her own nation, and Samson knew he could not trust her. Samson therefore is to blame in part for Delilah's betrayal of him. By far, the most clear-cut of the examples is that of David and Bathsheba. David saw Bathsheba, whom he knew to be a married woman, bathing on top of her roof and had her brought to his palace, where he slept with her. She conceived a child, and David sent her husband, his loyal supporter, out into the front lines of battle to be killed. As punishment for David's sin, God killed their child. Since the men Gawain mentions, David in particular, are all partly responsible for their own downfalls, Gawain's attempt to foist the blame for his sin onto the host's wife gains little credence from these biblical examples.

KEY FACTS

FULL TITLE
Sir Gawain and the Green Knight

AUTHOR
Anonymous; referred to as the Gawain-poet or the Pearl-poet

TYPE OF WORK
Alliterative poem

GENRE
Romance, Arthurian legend

LANGUAGE
Middle English (translated into modern English)

TIME AND PLACE WRITTEN
Ca. 1340–1400, West Midlands, England

PUBLISHER
The original work circulated for an unknown length of time in manuscript format. It now exists as MS Cotton Nero A.x, fols. 91r–124v, held at the British Library. Many different modern English and original-language editions exist.

NARRATOR
Third person omniscient

POINT OF VIEW
The Gawain-poet tells the story mainly from Gawain's point of view. However, he also occasionally narrates moments that happen outside the scope of Gawain's direct experience, most notably the host's daily hunts.

TONE
The narrator's tone toward Gawain's story hovers between straightforward praise and irony-tinged ambivalence. He occasionally refuses to give a straightforward account of characters' motives, leaving it ambiguous whether he approves or disapproves of the codes of courtly behavior and ethics that he describes. At times his tone can be nostalgic for the mythical past, but at other times he verges on criticizing a

former age that is neither innocent nor pure. He often achieves this level of ambiguity through the use of signs and symbols with undefined meanings.

TENSE

Past; some commentaries on the action in the present tense

SETTING (TIME)

The mythical past of King Arthur's court (sometime after Rome's fall, but before recorded history)

SETTINGS (PLACE)

Camelot; the wilderness; Bertilak's castle; the Green Chapel

PROTAGONIST

Sir Gawain

MAJOR CONFLICT

The major conflict is largely Gawain's struggle to decide whether his knightly virtues are more important than his life. Before he knows that the Green Knight has supernatural abilities, Gawain accepts the Green Knight's challenge to an exchange of blows. Once the Green Knight survives the blow, Gawain has a year and a day before he must seek out the Green Knight to receive the return blow, which will almost surely mean his own death. Once he has found the castle of a host who promises to show him the way to the Green Chapel, he struggles to protect and maintain his knightly virtues while remaining courteous to his host's wife, and he struggles to keep his pacts with the Green Knight and his host, despite his fear of death.

RISING ACTION

Gawain accepts the Green Knight's covenant and chops off the Green Knight's head, but he survives the blow. Two months before he is due to meet the knight for his own decapitation, Gawain sets out through the wilderness in search of the Green Chapel. He happens upon a castle, where he stays until he must leave for his challenge. At the castle, Gawain's courtesy, chastity, and honesty are all tempted. Gawain then journeys to confront the Green Knight at the Green Chapel.

CLIMAX

Gawain encounters the Green Knight at the Green Chapel. After feinting with his axe twice, the Green Knight strikes Gawain on the third swing, but only nicks his neck.

FALLING ACTION

The Green Knight explains all the mysteries of the story. He and Gawain's host at the castle are the same man, named Bertilak. Morgan le Faye, the old woman at the castle, is actually behind all the events of the story. Gawain admits his breach of contract in having kept the green girdle and promises to wear the girdle as a banner of his weakness.

THEMES

The nature of chivalry; the letter of the law

MOTIFS

The seasons; games

SYMBOLS

The pentangle; the green girdle

FORESHADOWING

The Green Knight's reiteration of Gawain's promise as he leaves Camelot foreshadows Gawain's eventual encounter with the knight. The description of the changing seasons at the beginning of Part 2 foreshadows Gawain's emotional development in the following parts. The strange, hallucinatory appearance of Bertilak's castle foreshadows the untrustworthy nature of its inhabitants. The lady's offer of a green girdle foreshadows Gawain's ability to cheat death.

KEY FACTS

Study Questions & Essay Topics

Study Questions

1. *The host's wife goes after the man she wants, and uses a great deal of rhetorical and argumentative skill to seduce him. To what extent would you describe the host's wife as a powerful or progressive female character?*

The host's wife appears to exercise a great deal of agency. Unlike Arthur's queen, Guinevere, who sits silently passive amidst the courtiers at Camelot, the lady of Hautdesert speaks, thinks, and acts. Gawain considers the host's wife even more attractive than Guinevere, and, clearly, the lady aims to give this impression—she wears revealing clothing that bares her breasts and back. She does her hair up elaborately, and it is possible to read line 952 as a statement that she wears makeup. The host's wife crawls directly into Gawain's bed once she has decided to seduce him, not waiting for him to come to her like a proper courtly lady.

In many ways, this lady seems more modern than a medieval woman. She chooses her lovers for herself and pursues her own desires, and she shows a keen ability to read people and a shrewd talent for arguing. When simple seduction fails to convince Gawain, she shows that she knows how to get under the knight's skin by questioning his reputation and accusing him of discourtesy. Also, she is literate: in lines 1512–1519, she mentions having read romances. The verbal battle that ensues between the lady and Gawain escalates in intensity every day, and it seems possible that she eventually would have won if Gawain hadn't left the castle. She shows herself to be every bit as clever at arguing as Gawain, if not more so.

Yet the Gawain-poet limits the lady in some interesting ways. First of all, he never gives her a name. Guinevere and Morgan le Faye, the other major female characters, both possess names, but the host's lady—arguably the most important of the three women—remains anonymous. Furthermore, we discover at the poem's end that the host's wife is not in fact her own agent. Though she clearly possesses beauty, intelligence, and skill, her use of all three is authorized and legitimized by her husband. To this extent, the lady acts on his behalf in seducing Gawain. In the most negative reading, Bertilak acts as his wife's pimp; in the most positive, the two act as partners. In any case, the lady does not act independently.

Of course, we also discover that Bertilak acts on behalf of Morgan le Faye, another woman. The most powerful agent in the story turns out to be a female character after all, but we learn so little about her and her motives that she remains as much of an enigma to us as Guinevere does. We don't even know the name of the female character we know best (the host's wife), and the other central female figures we know only as types (the beautiful queen, the evil witch). In his portrayals of women, the Gawain-poet exposes and subverts a variety of stereotypes, but his own opinion about how much agency women have or should have remains obscure.

2.   *What are the three reactions to Gawain's sin at the end of* Sir Gawain and the Green Knight? *How do they compare to one another?*

At the end of *Sir Gawain and the Green Knight*, we encounter opinions of how bad Gawain's sin really was from three sources: Bertilak, King Arthur, and Sir Gawain. Sir Gawain's view of his own sin seems harsh. When he realizes that the Green Knight and the host are the same man, Gawain curses himself, saying, "Accursed be a cowardly and covetous heart! / In you is villainy and vice, and virtue laid low!" (2374–2375). He proceeds to deprecate himself as a coward who has fallen short of his chivalric code. He calls himself a "faulty and false" knight (2382), and asks if he can regain the host's "good grace" (2387).

Though he initially chastises himself, Gawain goes on in lines 2411–2428 to recall several Bible stories about men who sin because of women. The host's wife exposed Gawain's flaws, he claims, just as Eve exposed Adam's, Delilah exposed Samson's, and Bathsheba exposed David's. Though Gawain couches his discussion of the "wiles of a woman" in terms of a woman's ability to make "a dullard . . . dote" (2414), he comes close to blaming the lady for his own downfall. Gawain decides to keep the girdle not only as a reminder of his fault, but as a sign for others, metaphorically equat-

ing himself with Cain (the son of Adam and Eve and the first mur-
derer) who bore a mark so that everyone could recognize him as a
sinner. Gawain's sin seems much less profound than Cain's, yet his
decision to wear the girdle as a "sign of excess" (2433) that recalls
"[t]he faults and the frailty of the flesh perverse" (2435) aligns him
with one of the greatest sinners in the Bible.

Arthur's reaction to Gawain's account of his sin differs radically
from Gawain's own. The Gawain-poet refers to Gawain's telling the
knights and ladies of Camelot about his encounter at the Green
Chapel as a confession of his "cares and discomfitures" (2494).
When Gawain unveils the scar and shows them the girdle, blushing
for shame, Arthur and his followers laugh out loud. For Gawain's
sake, all the knights and ladies take up the girdle as a symbol, wearing green silk baldrics on their arms. We might read this moment as
Arthur acknowledging that all men are sinners and, by sharing in
Gawain's misery, offering him comfort. On the other hand, there is
something too lighthearted about Arthur's response, which recalls
the youthful, inexperienced, jovial court in Part 1. Gawain has
clearly outgrown such an outlook, but Camelot essentially turns
Gawain's mark of weakness into a fashion statement.

By far, Bertilak has the most moderate of the three reactions. He
claims that Gawain's morally exceptional behavior impresses him,
even though Gawain kept the lady's gift of the girdle a secret. Bertilak says that the difference between Gawain and other knights is
like the difference between a pearl and peas. He admits that Gawain
has flaws, but he spares him from the fatal blow out of an apprecia-
tion for how well Gawain stood up to the tests. Though at first it
seems that Bertilak believes only in the letter of the law, in Part 4 he
shows a justice tempered with mercy. Bertilak is realistic about what
happened and therefore seems best suited of the three men to judge
the severity of Gawain's sin.

3. *Names—or a lack thereof—play an important role in* Sir
    Gawain and the Green Knight. *Discuss a few of the ways
    that the naming process or a name itself functions in
    the poem.*

The Gawain-poet investigates whether naming can fix, contain, or
transform physical reality, and names in the poem function in multiple ways. Proper nouns can contain or transfer reputation or status. For instance, at the beginning and the end of the poem, the
author refers to the way great cities are named. Rome is named for
Romulus, Tuscany is named for Ticius, Lombardy is named for Lan-
gaberd, and Britain is named for Brutus. By virtue of its name, Britain maintains a connection with ancient Troy, Brutus's native city. In
a related way, the Green Knight challenges Arthur's court, referring
to the "renown of the Round Table" (313). Later in the poem, the
lady uses a similar strategy when she claims that her "guest is not
Gawain" when she feels he has failed to live up to his reputation as
a courteous knight (1293). The poem shows that names can contain
reputation and transfer status; as such, a name must be defended
against defamation so that it can legitimize the power of that to
which (or whom) it refers.

As a concrete noun, a name can allow for a detailed knowledge of
a thing or a person. For instance, the Gawain-poet names the individual parts of Gawain's armor and uses the same technique when
describing the host's court, Arthur's feast, and the different parts of
each hunt. This kind of naming renders the poem tactile for the
reader, as we get to know certain things, processes, people, and
places intimately by knowing their specific names. Yet this kind of
knowledge juxtaposes the utter ineffability of other things, concepts, and people in the poem. For instance, the host, his wife, his
castle, and the old woman all remain nameless, adding to the sense
of suspense and foreboding surrounding them. We know how many
turrets the castle has, but we don't know the name of its lord. In this
way, names can reveal certain kinds of knowledge and expose certain kinds of ignorance regarding the physical world. Like the pentangle and the girdle, both of which are symbols whose meaning
fluctuates and refuses to remain stable throughout the course of the
poem, names prove to be empty signifiers. Ultimately, the Gawain-
poet points out that the name frequently fails to mediate between
objective reality and man's subjective comprehension of it.

SUGGESTED ESSAY TOPICS

1. Why might the Gawain-poet wish to frame his Arthurian, courtly romance within the context of classical epic?

2. What different ideological systems govern morality in *Sir Gawain and the Green Knight*? Do they seem to compete with one another, or do they overlap? Which systems appear to dominate by the end of the tale, and why?

3. What forms of love (brotherly love, spiritual love, courtly love, erotic love, and so forth) exist in the text, and in what types of relationships do they appear (friendships, marriages, relationships with God, and so forth)? Does love most commonly manifest itself as suffering or as ennoblement? Why do you think so many scholars analyze this text as part of the courtly love tradition?

4. In Part 4, the Green Knight and Gawain agree that all their problems can be blamed on women. Do you think we're meant to take the "woman blaming" ending seriously or to question it, and therefore (perhaps) to question the entire misogynist tradition to which Gawain alludes?

5. Many scenes and characters in *Sir Gawain and the Green Knight* are doubled or multiplied. Why do you think the writer structures his poem this way? What effect does the repetition of passages have on the reader? How does this formal element of poetic composition relate to what is happening at the content level? You might choose one doubled scene (like Gawain's departures from Camelot and Hautdesert) or character (Bertilak and the Green Knight) or something otherwise multiplied, like the "five fives" of Gawain's pentangle.

QUESTIONS & ESSAYS

REVIEW & RESOURCES

QUIZ

1. How long does Gawain stay at Bertilak's castle?

    A. All winter
    B. One night
    C. Eight days
    D. Three days

2. Who wrote *Sir Gawain and the Green Knight*?

    A. Geoffrey Chaucer
    B. An anonymous writer known as the Gawain-poet
    C. An anonymous writer known as the Unknown Poet
    D. J. R. R. Tolkien

3. What classical city is mentioned at the beginning and end of the poem?

    A. Troy
    B. Athens
    C. Jerusalem
    D. Sparta

4. During whose reign does the poem take place?

    A. King Richard II
    B. King Alfred
    C. Queen Elizabeth
    D. King Arthur

5. Next to whom does Gawain sit at the New Year's feast?

    A. Sir Bedivere
    B. Dame Ragnell
    C. Queen Guinevere
    D. Morgan le Faye

6.   What is the name of Gawain's horse?

    A.   Grendel
    B.   Incitatus
    C.   Gringolet
    D.   Secretariat

7.   What animal does the host hunt on the second day?

    A.   Boar
    B.   Deer
    C.   Bear
    D.   Fox

8.   What color is Gawain's surcoat?

    A.   Green
    B.   Black
    C.   Red
    D.   Silver

9.   Where is Gawain supposed to find the Green Knight?

    A.   The Green Castle
    B.   Hautdesert
    C.   Morgan le Faye's house
    D.   The Green Chapel

10.   What is the Green Knight's real name?

    A.   Bertilak de Hautdesert
    B.   Sir Bedivere of Camelot
    C.   Havelok the Dane
    D.   Grimpy the Hunchback

11.   What is Bertilak's wife's true name?

    A.   Lady Elaine
    B.   Dame Ragnell
    C.   She remains nameless
    D.   Morgan le Faye

12.   What four men does Gawain compare himself to in Part 4?

A.   Jesus, Joseph, James, and John
B.   Adam, Solomon, Samson, and David
C.   Brutus, Ticius, Romulus, and Aeneas
D.   Arthur, Bedivere, Lancelot, and Galahad

13.   How many points does the star on Gawain's shield have?

A.   8
B.   6
C.   3
D.   5

14.   What happens to the Green Knight's first axe?

A.   Gawain throws it into the lake
B.   He takes it with him, brandishing it as he leaves
     the hall
C.   Gawain and Arthur mount it on the wall as a souvenir
D.   The host uses it to kill the boar

15.   What love token does the lady first offer Gawain?

A.   A ring
B.   Her bra
C.   Her girdle
D.   A glove

16.   How much time does Gawain have to locate the
      Green Knight?

A.   Exactly one year
B.   Exactly six months
C.   Exactly one year and eight days
D.   Exactly one year and one day

17.   Which of the following is an example of alliteration?

A.   The rain in Spain falls mainly in the plain
B.   We were the first that ever burst / Into that silent sea
C.   In pious times, ere priestcraft did begin, / Before
        polygamy was made a sin
D.   True men pay what they owe; / No danger then
        in sight

18.   What weapon does the Green Knight have in Part 4?

A.   A Sumerian scimitar
B.   A Danish axe
C.   A French bayonet
D.   A Lancaster lance

19.   During what century was *Sir Gawain and the Green Knight*
        composed?

A.   The fourteenth
B.   The thirteenth
C.   The sixteenth
D.   The eleventh

20.   Why does Gawain refuse the lady's advances?

A.   Because the chivalric code requires him to
        remain chaste
B.   Because she is married
C.   Because he aspires to the values represented
        by the pentangle
D.   All of the above

21.   How many kisses does Gawain receive from the lady on the
        second day?

A.   3
B.   1
C.   2
D.   5

22. What is the name of the court where Gawain first meets the Green Knight?

   A. Troy
   B. Camelot
   C. Hautdesert
   D. Xanadu

23. What is Gawain's relationship to King Arthur?

   A. He is Arthur's son
   B. He is Arthur's brother
   C. He is Arthur's tarot card reader
   D. He is Arthur's nephew

24. Why does Gawain take the lady's green girdle?

   A. Because he doesn't want to die
   B. Because he wants to give it to the Green Knight as a gift
   C. Because he is overcome with desire
   D. Because she threatens to kill him

25. What does Bertilak's castle appear to be made of when Gawain first sees it?

   A. Fox pelts
   B. Danish stone
   C. Paper
   D. Gold

ANSWER KEY:
1: C; 2: B; 3: A; 4: D; 5: C; 6: C; 7: A; 8: C; 9: D; 10: A; 11: D; 12: B; 13: D; 14: C; 15: A; 16: D; 17: C; 18: B; 19: B; 20: C; 21: D; 22: B; 23: D; 24: A; 25: C

SUGGESTIONS FOR FURTHER READING

ANONYMOUS. *The Complete Works of the Pearl Poet*. Ed. Casey
Finch. Berkeley: University of California Press, 1993.

BREWER, DEREK, AND JONATHON GIBSON. *Companion to the
Gawain-poet*. Rochester, New York: D. S. Brewer, 1997.

BREWER, ELISABETH. Sir Gawain and the Green Knight: *Sources
and Analogues*. Rochester, New York: D. S. Brewer, 1992.

BURROW, J. A. *The Gawain-poet*. Plymouth, Massachusetts:
Northcote House, 2000.

LEWIS, C. S. *The Discarded Image*. Cambridge: Cambridge
University Press, 1964.

SPEARING, A. C. *The Gawain Poet: A Critical Study*. Cambridge:
Cambridge University Press, 1970.

STAINSBY, MEG. Sir Gawain and the Green Knight: *An
Annotated Bibliography, 1978–1989*. New York: Garland
Publishers, 1992.

A Note on the Type

The typeface used in SparkNotes study guides is Sabon, created by master typographer Jan Tschichold in 1964. Tschichold revolutionized the field of graphic design twice: first with his use of asymmetrical layouts and sanserif type in the 1930s when he was affiliated with the Bauhaus, then by abandoning assymetry and calling for a return to the classic ideals of design. Sabon, his only extant typeface, is emblematic of his latter program: Tschichold's design is a recreation of the types made by Claude Garamond, the great French typographer of the Renaissance, and his contemporary Robert Granjon. Fittingly, it is named for Garamond's apprentice, Jacques Sabon.

SPARKNOTES
TEST PREPARATION
GUIDES

The SparkNotes team figured it was time to cut standardized tests down to size. We've studied the tests for you, so that SparkNotes test prep guides are:

Smarter:
Packed with critical-thinking skills and test-
taking strategies that will improve your score.

Better:
Fully up to date, covering all new features of the tests,
with study tips on every type of question.

Faster:
Our books cover exactly what you need to
know for the test. No more, no less.

SparkNotes Study Guides: